LIBERATION FROM TYRANNY

RONNI KOVE

ANAPHORA LITERARY PRESS

ATLANTA, GEORGIA

Anaphora Literary Press
1803 Treehills Parkway
Stone Mountain, GA 30088
http://anaphoraliterary.com

Book design by Anna Faktorovich, Ph.D.

Copyright © 2014 by Ronni Kove

All rights reserved. No part of this book may be reproduced in any form or by any electronic or mechanical means, including information storage and retrieval systems, without permission in writing from Ronni Kove. Writers are welcome to quote brief passages in their critical studies, as American copyright law dictates.

Pixaby Images: Beagle Resting on a Chesterfield Sofa; Happy Jumping Man; Horse Pasture; Lupinien Nature in New Zealand; Motorcycle Stuntman; Rose Flowers; Rummelsburg Bay Berlin Winter Ice Skater; Sunset Evening Sky; Tree at Dawn: Bucovina Romania; White-Breasted Nuthatch.

Published in 2014 by Anaphora Literary Press

Liberation from Tyranny
Ronni Kove—1st edition.

ISBN-13: 978-1-937536-87-9
ISBN-10: 1-937536-87-4

Library of Congress Control Number: 2014951079

LIBERATION FROM TYRANNY

RONNI KOVE

CONTENTS

PART 1: NATURE REVIVES — 7
Gift of the Valley — 8
The Creek — 9
Fluttering of Wings of Joy — 10
Flying — 11
The Tiny Bird — 12
The Field — 13
The Glow — 14
Explore — 15
Camp Nights — 16
Spring — 17
Winter — 18
Days for Adventure — 19
Tree — 20

PART 2: LEADERS OF HUMANITY — 21
The First Lady — 22
A Monumental Man — 23
Mother Theresa — 24
A Real Princess — 25
Peace — 26
Civil Rights — 27

PART 3: PEOPLE: GOOD AND EVIL — 28
The Quads My Favorites — 29
The Forgotten Soul — 30
The Boss from Hell — 31
Co-Workers — 32
True Americans — 33
The Blissful Aunt — 34
Memorial for Louise — 35
My Man — 36
Action Speaks — 37
No Humanity — 38
Willie the Quadruplet — 39
Retail — 40

PART 4: LOVE FOR ANIMALS — 41
Native to Our Country — 42
Cocoa the Chihuahua — 43

Pals	45
Sally the Beagle	46
Buddy the Basset	47
Memorial for Sally	48
Mysterious	49

PART 5: CLOSENESS OF RELATIONSHIPS	**50**
Best Friend	51
Sisters	52
Pain Deep Inside	53
The Break Up	54
Make UP	55
Daughter and Mother	56
Happy Anniversary	57

PART 6: EMOTIONAL STATES	**58**
Floating on a Cloud	59
Free from Pain	60
No Explanation Needed	61
I Am Here	62
Help	63
Soul Searching	64
No Return	65

PART 7: SPORTS HEALING	**66**
Playing	67
Contentment	68
A Sport	69
Ballet on Ice	70
Invigorating	71
The Lake	72

PART 8: INSPIRING	**73**
Love	74
Getting Better	75
Hope	76
Talent of the Heart	77
Dependent	78
Liberation from Tyranny	79
I Prayed for Help	80
Guardian Angel	81
Gift	82

PART 1

Nature Revives

THE GIFT OF THE VALLEY

The mountains sculpture the land
Breath taking views
Bring sweet tranquility
Beauty beyond the imagination
Cows that catch the sun
The sunset softens the soul
The corn fields are thriving
Making nature bounteous
The geese paint the sky
Rolling fields, hills and pastures
It has an intensity that fills the heart
A picturesque panorama
Enchanting colorful visions
Brilliantly enlightens
The trail connects man to nature
The creek cultivates the land
This scenery is beyond sight
Where the land meets the sky
A gentle touch of paradise
All senses are so keenly felt
God's cherished gift
For all to behold
The valley is for eternity

THE CREEK

Water running so freely
Reflections of trees so vividly
Time stands still
While beautiful thoughts transcend
The air is so fresh and sweet
The geese fly in patterns
The cows graze lustfully
The colorful fish swim
Spreading nature's hand
The creek becomes alive

FLUTTERING WINGS OF JOY

Spreading multi-colors
Metamorphosis beyond the imagination
Creating a paradise
Enhances nature's beauty
A sight of fascination
Sets the scene for contentment
As it sours through the flowers
Flying so gracefully
An angel in flight
God's spectacular creation

FLYING

Gliding through the air
That is not rare
Big wings that spread
That is as soothing as a bed
He takes over the beach
That is not out of reach
Colors of white and grey
Like a sunny day
He sings a song
That will last long
He stays by the bay
Like blooming roses of May
He is very pleasing
While he is teasing
He is so peaceful
Yet very beautiful
He wears a crown
He goes to town
The seagulls will reign

THE TINY BIRD

Smallest bird
Have you heard?
The fluttering of the wings
It sounds like the bird sings
A bird so unique
With a very long beak
It sucks nectar from flowers
It flies above towers
It's a beautiful sight
It's as graceful as a kite
Everyone wants to see
It opens doors with a key
It's humming is soothing
It's so fabulously moving
I want to see a humming bird

THE FIELD

Nature is so serene
While I felt so keen
Trees all around
You aren't bound
You can fly like a bird
With boldness of a herd
A new sense of being
With great meaning
The body feels so light
That is definitely right
Enlighten is the game
Where all thoughts are the same
Freedom beyond belief
Oh! What a relief
A feeling never felt before
One could not ignore
Standing in the field
Feeling God's creations

THE GLOW

A hidden space
It's my place
I sat there
Because the lake is near
Beauty that touched me
That's the only way to be
As the sky sets
The orange forms nets
Vivid reflections of the light
Before the night
The soul is soothed
I was intensely moved
Nature's sweet touch
That means very much
Contentment is in my reach
Like the waves of a beach
I never want to leave
The clearing is a retreat
The sunset is mesmerizing

EXPLORE

Walking through the woods
Causing mixed moods
It appears to be water
That looks like mortar
There is a blanket of green
That isn't difficult to be seen
There is a sense of doom
That brings on gloom
It raises your eye
That causes you to sigh
There is an intense fascination
That causes such a strong manifestation
There is Stillness
 Lifelessness
 Quietness
What is this?
It's a swamp

CAMP NIGHTS

During the night
The beauty was out of sight
The lights around the lake
Were like icing on a cake
The swimming fish
Were like a colorful dish
Music that had a soft tone
As I sat alone
I sat there on the dock
Feeling solid like a rock
I want to stay forever
But that surely is never
The lake shines always

SPRING

Array of flowers blooming
Trees come alive
Rolling fields of green shades
Sweet smell of nature
Birds sing there joy
Children play in the park
Colors that exhibit paradise
Life is rekindled
As the stream flows into the creek
The creek flows into the river
The growth is endless
The warmth is refreshing
Beauty has been born

WINTER

White crystals fall from heaven
Cool whispers of wind
Birds have lost their song
The fields have a white glow
The chimes are musical
The trees lacking color
Animals are sleeping
The crickets have been subdued
Nature is resting

DAYS FOR ADVENTURE

Nights of sparkling stars
Sweet fragrance of flowers blooming
Nature grows vigorously
Mountains are so majestic
Foliage forms patterns of color
Canaries sing its beauty
Time for tranquility
Free as the sky above
Running by the sunset
Swimming sets new horizons
As the waves go back and forth
Summer heats the soul

THE TREE

It starts so very tiny
Than grows in all directions
With twists and turns
It's intricate and complicated in character
It has so much detail and history
There are many obstacles
Dealing with the elements
Changing with the seasons
Branches have a variety of shapes
Not one branch is the same
The leaves finish the tree
Color that enhances life
It has beauty that is so simple
No one knows its destiny
The tree withers away
It grows no more leaves
But wait a seed is sprouting
That is the cycle of life
God's creation for all

PART 2

Leaders of Humanity

THE FIRST LADY

She was so shy
She could not say hi
She had no self esteem
But her face did beam
She became a great speaker
Oh!!! What a keeper
Her speeches hit like a storm
Thank God she was born
She traveled all over
Spreading a soft cover
She loved people
Like the beauty of a church steeple
Her words spread like a butterfly
Their weight flew high
Thank you Eleanor

A MONUMENTAL MAN

He was striving
So that his people were thriving
He set his people free
Like the growth of a tree
He had done many sacrifices
He had no vices
He did blow his horn
He was a great leader for very long
He asked for nothing
Yet he was something
He was a great example
Like his fight against the British was ample
He was as strong as the sun
Because he did not run
He pulled the country together
That was for the better
He held no political function
Yet his cast was a great reduction
He will never be forgotten
The father of India

MOTHER THERESA

She did great deeds
To help people with many needs
She cared for the ill
By using more than a pill
Sick came first
Because they felt the worst
She is a heroine of the heart
Because she did more than her part
She wanted to give
So that many could live
She brought lots of smiles
That traveled for miles
She made the sad
Not feel so bad
She gave people hope
Like John Paul II the Pope
She nurtures everybody
Even those that felt like nobody
She healed their soul
That made them whole
She is faithful to the lord
With a great accord
Thank God for the blessed mother
There could be no other

A REAL PRINCESS

Her inner beauty radiated from her face
Her life was cut short by a chase
She is loved by all
Like a high bouncing ball
Her legend will live on forever
No one would say; never
She bloomed like a flower
That influenced with great power
Her smile was so bright
Her bonds were tight
When she laughed out loud
That chased away a cloud
She was so sweet
Like her heart would beat
She was the most liked in the palace
She had no malice
Royalty was her game
Her love for people was the same
Her memory will live on

PEACE

Time to grow
While the people will glow
People will live
So they can give
Like a bright sunny day
Depicts a sweet lily in May
The angels will sing
Like a sparkling diamond ring
Celebrate the glory
It is an endless story
Great times to reminisce
With much significance
The end of war
Who could ask for anything more
Instead of the color red
Good times ahead
Killing is over
It is now time to recover
Countless lives were lost
At a very great cost
John Lennon knew war was bad
That it made everyone very sad
He preached for peace
Hopefully his dream will come true

CIVIL RIGHTS

Such a kind face
Not against any race
He was a good man
With a great plan

Equality was his game
That gave him so much fame
His principles are the best
That laid slavery to rest

The war caused much pain
With many days of rain
"Let freedom ring"
The African American can sing

His heart was stabbed with knives
For the soldiers that lost their lives
He stood tall
Above it all

He had character
With great stature
He stood for the constitution
Oh what a solution

He could write
That was out of sight
Thanks to Abe
He greatly gave
"By the people, for the people"

PART 3

People: Good and Evil

THE QUADS MY FAVORITES

The special, awesome and spectacular four
Their love you want more
They are so tight
Their closeness reaches a great height
Their understanding of each other
While they were born together
They spoke their own words
The songs of chirping birds

They know each other so well
The sounds of a ringing bell
Their music will play
The tunes will always stay
They grow together as branches of a tree
The glow their eyes will see
The horses will gallop even better
As their souls will stay together

Blissfulness they will bring
That makes my heart sing
Their mutual love
Depicts the flight of a dove
I love you all more than words can express

THE FORGOTTEN SOUL

Wondering with no destination
Lost from the world
Eyes are hopeless
Voice is not heard
Sadness is deep
Thoughts of confusion
Elements are so harsh
Strength to survive
Days are so long
Starvation is evident
Depiction of loneliness
Desires are very simple
This predicament is for all
Why has society forgotten the homeless man?

THE BOSS FROM HELL

Contempt is all that is uttered from his lips
Respect is universes away
Words of wisdom are not apparent
Disdain is his game
Understanding is not in his realm
Power is his only friend
Controlling is his tool
Appreciation is beyond his existence
Scorn is his only voice
Save me from this boss from Hell

CO-WORKERS

Mocking is their style
Disloyalty to the extreme
Sincerity non existent
Insecurity is their mode
Insensitivity is their weapon
Class is beyond their reach
Gossip is their excitement
Egos with attitudes
Talking is irrelevant
I am blissful that I have far better CHARACTER

TRUE AMERICANS

They were here first
But they were treated as the last
Their land was taken
Oh were they shaken
Their culture is so fine
Like a smooth glass of wine
They cultivated the land
Yet they didn't have a hand
Their forced into flight
Where they are out of sight
They offered so much
With a gentle touch
They were forgotten
As though they were rotten
Their soul is lost
At a great cost
The Native American is our heritage

THE BLISSFUL AUNT

We are many miles apart
We are still close in heart
We miss each other
It will not be over
You are all
Like colorful leaves of fall
You are all like sunrays
That always fills my days
When you call
I have a ball
Thank God for family
I love you all blissfully
You are so deep in my soul
Like a bottomless bowl
You are all in my heart
That is more than a start

MEMORIAL FOR LOUISE

She was the best
Now she can rest
She suffered many years
That brought lots of tears
She was a sensitive person
That caused lots of sun
She was so kind
But she was in a bind
She was soft spoken
Her heart was broken
She was a great mother
Her goodness spread like a cover
Now she is blissful
She is not tearful
In heaven she will be
Now she will see
Louise has gone to the light

MY MAN

He has a sense of humor
That is not a rumor
He is very smart
He offers his part
He can talk
More than most can walk
He is such a child
That's making it mild
He likes to have fun
As bright as the sun
Coins are his expertise
While he likes to tease
There is no shame
In playing his game
His love is strong
What could be wrong?
He is so cute
Like the songs of a flute
He is the child inside the man

ACTION SPEAKS

He cares since I was born
Like the sound of a loud horn
Listening is his way
To everything I say
He is so great
He has no hate
He is so very kind
He helps me out of a bind
Our memories are beautiful
He is wonderful
He was always there
Yet he had a lot to bear
He has given me great advice
That is very nice
We are so close
Like the beauty of a rose
I love you Dad

NO HUMANITY

Jealousy turns into hate
What a bad fate
One is blind
To mankind
Evil takes hold
That is so very cold
Millions have died
The killers have lied
Compassion flies away
Another tragic day
Help is not insight
They could not fight
The flowers will not bloom
There is a big tomb
There was a black mist
Like a pounding fist
The tears will flow
Their souls will not glow
This can get worse
Like a horrible curse
We must not let this happen again!!!

WILLIE THE QUADRUPLET

He had it rough
But he was very tough
He was just so tiny
He had a cute hinny
He could not play
The sun did not have a ray
His breathing was weak
He was unable to speak
Many times he was rushed to the intensive care
He had too much to bear
Two years he was intensely ill
That could not be cured with just a pill
He could not eat
His autism caused a hot seat
His childhood was bad
That makes me mad
He now shines like a star
He has come so far
He is so very special
Thank you God for saving my Willie

RETAIL

Customers can be so rude
Why do they intrude?
I am so polite
Even when I am right
I want to scream
Because they are so mean
They sting like a bee
I just want to flee
They have all the power
Like falling from a tower
Their voices are scorn
While they blow their horn
Their attitude is so poor
Who could ignore
Their tongue is as sharp as a razor
Save me from these nasty people

PART 4

Love for Animals

NATIVE TO OUR COUNTRY

So grand that it is vividly beautiful
So picturesque when outlined by the sunset
A thick magical wooly coat
It portrays a mammoth appearance

Innocent and docile
It has no greed
It has no jealousy
It has no bias
It has no dishonesty

It used to roam freely
Now it's behind fences
It has committed no crime
It was here before our time
Their numbers have been greatly diminished
It has almost been finished
Why does man kill the buffalo?

COCOA THE CHIHUAHUA

He wags his tail
That makes a sweet trail
He is such a cutie
Oh what a beauty

Even though he is adorable
He is also lovable
He is such a prize
With no demise

He has a friendly bark
Like the songs of a lark
He is loyal
He is Royal

He is a bundle of joy
He is a playful boy
He is so tame
And plays a fun game

He can run
And have so much fun
He is the greeter
What could be neater?

He is so smart
With a great heart
He is the best
Better than the rest

He is so small
Like a little ball
He is a little guy
More than money could buy
Don't you just love him?

PALS

They stick together like glue
A present for me and you
They are so close
When they touch nose to nose
They cuddle together
Nothing could be better
They use each other for pillows
Like two sleeping willows
Together they are so cute
As they grow together like a root
They have different voices
While they have similar choices
They meow or bark
Like candles in the dark
They are such opposites
Yet great composites
They trust each other
Like a brother
They keep each other clean
Instead of being mean
They love each other to the end
They will never bend
They are so tender
As they are the sender
Together they play
With each other all day
They dance the same tune
Like the light of a moon

SALLY THE BEAGLE

She was stricken with pain
That caused tears like rain
Like a loud sound
She was bound
She is so fearful
It gives you a tearful
She lost her voice
She did not have a choice
She is so strong
Even though she was treated wrong

She is so dear
Especially when she is near
She is such a joy
When she plays with a toy
She is so sweet
As she is great to meet

She feels good at home
She need not roam
She has a beautiful face
She keeps in tune with the pace
She is the lady of the hour
That is female dog power

BUDDY THE BASSET

He is so delightful
He talks a mouthful
He is so bashful

He is confused
Because he was abused
He felt very used

Now he is free
As a tall tree
He will lie on your knee

He is so lean
But he is not mean
Yet he is so keen

He is so tough
But does not play rough
Even though he has had enough

He is so sweet
He barks with a beat
He is so neat

Let's rejoice in his blissfulness
Buddy you made it
We love you Buddy

MEMORIAL FOR SALLY

She was so sweet
She played a good beat
She had many troubles
Now she fly's like bubbles
She went to heaven
Oh!!! What a haven
She now sings a song
She was very strong
She is looking from above
With lots of love
She can now bark
She has made her mark
She was so very special
Now she really is at peace
We love you Sally

MYSTERIOUS

Fur that shines
Soft and silky
Yellow marble eyes
Beauty that never fades

Leaping and jumping
Appearing and disappearing
Hunter by nature
Marks her territory

Keen senses
Magical intuition
Observant curiosity
Intelligent beyond belief

A powerful voice
Loving and affectionate
A soothing purr
That displays her personality

The black cat brings warmth and excitement into the home.

PART 5

Closeness of Relationships

BEST FRIEND

Multi colored buds
Soft light in the night
Deep unconditional understanding
The glow between us never dies
Sunshine on a dismal day
Music to my soul
Sweet memories not forgotten
Tender acts of kindness
Caring for eternity
What are best friends for?

SISTERS

A deep understanding
Closeness that fills the heart
Respect is miles long
Trust is never questioned
A bond that is solid
Memories are cherished
Fun times are endless
A relationship that is for eternity
Loyalty has no bounds
In life and death
As years go by
Sisters will always be sisters

PAIN IS DEEP INSIDE

The candle is not bright
Description of trees dying
When the birds don't sing
Darkness is all around
The days are cloudy
The nights are cold and lonely

But angels are near
The bond will never be broken
Part of you is lost forever
Sorrow that is incredibly overwhelming
Tears that can fill oceans
Everyday thoughts of a loved one
May he at peace
I will always miss him
The love never dies

THE BREAK UP

He broke my heart
That was a dreadful start
I felt like I lost me
Like a violent sea
The angels did not follow
I was filled with much sorrow
There was a weight on my shoulders
Like huge falling boulders
I roll down a hill
Like a slow turning mill
The pain is so real
Like a wounded seal
Sadness is beyond belief
I need some relief
Alone feels like forever
When he said never
My soul was stolen
Because I was broken
He was so very cruel
Like a stupid mule
He played a mean game
Which I could not tame
He ripped me apart
Like a master of an evil art
He will not win

MAKE UP

Sweet nothings whispered in my ear
He helps to save me from fear
Purring like a cat
Not blind as a bat
Leaves are on the trees
While I get off my knees
Sweet kisses
No misses
Tranquility I contemplate
It is so very great
My heart is filled with gold
While love is so bold
While the flowers bloom
I have left the tomb

We are so very tight
Like a night with light
He has a soothing touch
He gives me so much
There are so many sunny days
He helps me in so many ways
We are together again
There is no more rain
I am so happy thanks to him

DAUGHTER AND MOTHER

They liked the same things
As the church bells rings
Their love never dies
As the twinkle in their eyes
As the birds fly
Spreading sweet songs so high
Their souls are filled with love
As the soft white color of a dove
HER SPIRIT FLYS UP
Her life was like a full cup
She will look down
Hoping you will not frown
There were many good times
More than this poem that rhymes
Mom will always be close at heart

HAPPY ANNIVERSARY

The love they share
Is because they care
They are so very close
Like the delicate simplicity of a rose
Their trust is so very deep
They will surely keep
There memories travel far
Their love will shine like a star
They are a heavenly match
Oh!!! What a catch
He brings a sparkle to her eyes
That causes his heart to rise
They have been together very long
Like the cardinals singing their song
They are together as husband and wife
They have a great life

PART 6

Emotional States

FLOATING ON A CLOUD

The mind is so mysterious
Deep inner realizations
The truth lies beneath
Thoughts are alive
Visions passing by
People fade and reappear
Perplexed by images
Sights never seen before
Magical unpredictable events
Imagination runs wild
Creating a wonder land
Walking through a maze
Stories that are unreal
Time has no meaning
Fantasies are reborn
Please don't wake me!!!

FREE FROM PAIN

Not knowing how to feel
And yet it does not seem real
Like a dark cloud
As a voice so loud
She looked like she was sleeping
Yet I was weeping
The sun stopped shinning
Yet it was such poor timing
I felt doom
Like a hidden moon
She took her last breath
That was her death
Frozen emotion
When she stopped her motion
Her time had arrived

NO EXPLANATION NEEDED

Listening to all that is said
Soothing words of wisdom
Never interrupting comments
Believing the truth
Being sensitive to ones feelings
The soul is replenished
Angels are flying near by
As assistance is given
No more torment
The abuse is terminated
Rainbows cover the sky
Content is all around
Thank you for understanding my pain

I AM HERE

A place to rest
In your own little nest
Protected by these four walls
Even the halls
It's cozy
Like cheeks that are rosy
Everyone needs one
So you don't have to run
It's a serene haven
Not like a black raven
Privacy is here
Like a docile deer
I am finally home

HELP

People are so far away
What a quiet day
I just want to speak
All I can do is seek
Waking up alone
No need for the phone
I have so much sorrow
It will not change tomorrow
Please listen to me
I feel stung by a bee
It hurts so much
I have been out of touch
A friendly face
Like eloquent lace
I just want someone who cares

SOUL SEARCHING

It's not monetary
It's not prestige
It's not power
It's not class
It's not occupation
It's not intelligence

It is character
It is ability to love
It is compassion
It is sensitivity
It is sacrifice
It is spirituality

An inner realization
You tried with all your ability
When your soul is at peace
Now you have success

NO RETURN

When you say goodbye
The spirit flies high
The song never ends
Like fashionable trends
The angels appear
The soul does not disappear
There is a bright light
Even all night
You float
Not on a boat
You are not sad
Nor are you mad
You sense the unknown
You do not feel alone
The love you feel
Is so real
Peace has come
You don't feel numb
God will take care of you

PART 7

Sports Healing

PLAYING

To hit par
You would be a star
To hit the ball in the ruff
That would be tough
To hit a bogie
It's greater than a hoagie
To hit a birdie
Is as great as being a sweetie
To hit off the tee
Is like hitting to the sea
To hit to the green
It Is fun to be seen
To reach the hole
You are on a roll
Club power is out of sight
Let's play golf

CONTENTMENT

Fresh air running through your hair
The water is so serene and vibrant
It mesmerizes your thoughts
The waves hit the boat
Causing small rainbows
Colorful sails light up the bay
As they help glide the boat
 When they catch the wind
As the boat heels it is so exciting
The view is so scenic and calming
As the land is so far away
Let's go sailing

A SPORT

Swinging straight
To have the best rate
To get the ball
You do not have to be tall
Hit the ball over the net
You are surely set
Speed is the game
For all it's the same
The racket hits so smooth
While you have a great move
It is so intense
It makes so much sense
To win a match
Is a great catch
To play doubles
Causes no troubles
Singles is the way
I must say
The competition is so very strong
It has been for very long
Tennis any one

BALLET ON ICE

Gliding on ice
It's so very nice
Spinning in the air
Without a care
It paints a picture
More than just a sketch of a character
It is a beautiful art
That is more than being smart
It is moving
As well as soothing
Leaping high
While you give a sigh

It's invigorating
It's exciting
It's dancing
It's relaxing
Let's catch an eye full

INVIGORATING

You feel so lite
The sun is so bright
There are many strokes
Even for the old folks
The water is so serene
Each muscle used is so keen
You keep cool
While you swim in a pool
Good way to get out of the heat
While moving to the beat
Relaxing is an open book
While your mind is off the hook
All body parts are used
While you are so amused
Get off your towel

THE LAKE

Paddling along
Like a fast song
Almost pictures a race
At a rapid pace
As you float
While gliding in a boat
An amazing scene
That is so keen
This sport has charm
That is no alarm
What you have seen
Will cause you to be so serene
Paddling along
Just singing a song
It's stimulating
Yet relaxing
Kayaking is so much blissfulness

PART 8

Inspiring

LOVE

Sweetness of roses blooming
The larks sing loves glory
It's for all to behold
It has warmth that embraces all
The kindness enhances life
The truth will set you free
The glow will save your soul
It's like vines climbing endlessly
The intensity is powerful
Depicts the sky with rainbows
The music is in harmony
Angels dancing to loves tune
Rejoice in love's inner beauty

Tender as the night
Soft as the day
Love prevails

GETTING BETTER

The sunshine brings joy
You find a new awakening
Health brings a gleam to your eyes
As nature is so vivid
Enlightenment to your soul
It will set you free
Your song comes from heaven
While the body dances to wellness

HOPE

The candle is bright
You will see the light
When you feel sorrow
There will always be tomorrow
The lord works in ways
To help you through your days
Your face will glow
Like a beautiful bow
There will be a light in your eyes
Your spirits will rise
Always have hope
When you are at your last rope

TALENT OF THE HEART

So powerful
Yet not plentiful
So dear
Yet not near
Where is the caring?
Where is the giving?
Acts of kindness
Kindness is the ultimate

DEPENDENT

I cannot walk
But I can talk
I feel helpless
I am so restless
It is so hard to do
When I need you
I am so terrified
This made me stupefied
I need to take care of things
Like Angels fluttering there wings
Home is cold
While my afflicted body has such a hold
I will never give up

LIBERATION FROM TYRANNY

Kindness is rampant
Maturity fills the room
Going from sadness to blissfulness
Teamwork engulfs the soul
Peacefulness travels all around
A bright light is always lit
Colorful talk is evident
Flowers blooming endlessly
Sweet smell of beauty
Fun times are powerfully felt
Such great salvation
From working for the Salvation Army

I PRAYED FOR HELP

This vision is very real
What a fantastic deal
I sensed something
It sure wasn't anything
She knew all that I thought
A surprise that cannot be bought
She taught me new things
Like the chime that rings
She did appear to know
Beyond the falling snow
She helped me
Now I can see
She gave me advice
That was very nice
She used a great metaphor
Who could ask for anything more?
I asked for help for my nephew Willie
He is as beautiful as a lily
As you get better
He will recover faster
She came from above
She brought much love
She appeared
Then she disappeared
She was the presence of God
Thank you, guardian angel

GUARDIAN ANGEL

Is watching over you
Protecting you
Healing you
Inspiring you
Blessing you
Thinking of you
Hoping for you
Praying for you
You are always in my prayers and thoughts
Just like your Guardian Angel

GIFT

Open the box
It appears empty
Look deep inside
There is loyalty
There is sincerity
There is understanding
There is love
It's priceless
The most precious gift
Gift of the heart

OTHER ANAPHORA LITERARY PRESS TITLES

PLJ: Interviews with Best-Selling YA Writers
Editor: Anna Faktorovich

Inversed
By: Jason Holt

Notes on the Road to Now
By: Paul Bellerive

Devouring the Artist
By: Anthony Labriola

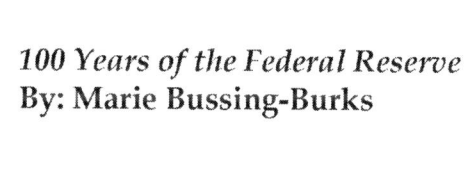

100 Years of the Federal Reserve
By: Marie Bussing-Burks

River Bends in Time
By: Glen A. Mazis

Interview with Larry Niven
Editor: Anna Faktorovich

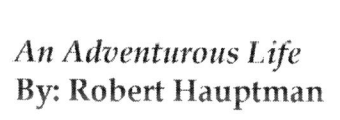

An Adventurous Life
By: Robert Hauptman